How to Start and Run a Successful Guitar Repair Business:

Practical Tips for the New Entrepreneur

By Jonny Blackwood

How to Start and Run a Successful Guitar Repair Business:
Practical Tips for the New Entrepreneur

By Jonny Blackwood

Other Books in this Series:
How to Setup Your Guitar like a Pro
How to Build and Setup Guitar Kits like a Pro

Available in Print and Digital Versions

Limit of Liability/Disclaimer of Warranty Notice: While the publisher and author have used their best efforts in preparing this book, they make no representations or warranties with respect to the accuracy or completeness of the contents of this book and specifically disclaim any implied warranties of merchantability or fitness for a particular purpose. No warranty may be created or extended by sales representatives or written sales materials. The advice and strategies contained herein may not be suitable for your situation. You should consult with a professional where appropriate. Neither the publisher, author or authors shall be liable for any loss of profit or any other commercial damages, including but not limited to special, incidental, consequential, or other damages.

Published by Learn-GuitarSetups.com
Contact email: info@learn-guitarsetups.com

Copyright 2016 Jonny Blackwood. All rights reserved. All trademarks and copyrighted material are the property of their respective owners. Images and graphics used courtesy of their respective owners. All rights reserved. No part of this book covered by copyrights hereon may be reproduced or copied in any manner whatsoever without written permission, except in the case of brief quotations embodied in articles and reviews. For information contact the publishers.

ISBN-13: 978-1542896474
ISBN-10: 1542896479

Published Feb. 1, 2017

Disclaimer
All trademarks, service marks, trade names and copyrights present in this book are trademarks, registered trademarks, or copyrights of their respective owners. Fender®, Strat®, Stratocaster®, Telecaster®, Tele®, P-Bass®, and J-Bass® are registered trademarks of Fender Musical Instruments Corporation. Floyd Rose® is a registered trademark of Floyd Rose Industries. Gibson® and Les Paul® are registered trademarks of Gibson Guitar Corp. Gretsch® is a registered trademark of Fred Gretsch® Enterprises. Learn-GuitarSetups.com, it's agents or authors are not affiliated with Fender®, Gibson®, Gretsch®, Floyd Rose®, or any other Brand, copyright or trademark listed in this Book. No warranty of any kind applies. Information in this book is for educational purposes only and the publisher, author, website owner, affiliates, and any other person associated with the distribution, marketing or advertising of this book publication will not be held liable for any damages of any kind as a result of action taken from the content within this book. The information contained in this book is provided in good faith by the author for general guidance on matters of interest only. All Rights Reserved.

TABLE OF CONTENTS

INTRODUCTION 4
GETTING STARTED 5
DAY IN THE LIFE OF RUNNING A GUITAR SHOP 5
SPECIALIZING, FINDING YOUR NICHE 8
    Service Sheet Example #1 with optional add-ons 9
YOUR TRAINING & EXPERIENCE 11
THE BUSINESS & HOW TO PROFIT 12
    Additional Revenue Streams 14
MARKUPS, MAPS, and YOUR COMPETITIVE EDGE 17
INCREASING YOUR STREET CREDIBILITY 18
SETTING UP SHOP: A Simple Process to Getting You Started 20
BUSINESS PLANS 22
BUSINESS STRUCTURES 23
TYPICAL STARTUP BUSINESS COSTS 26
YOUR POLICIES 28
ACCOUNTING SYSTEMS & RECORD KEEPING 31
MARKETING 34
ADVERTISING 36
CONCLUSION 42
RESOURCES 43
    Tools List 43
    Supplies List 44
    Equipment & Fixtures List 45
    Service Pricing Sheet EXAMPLE #1 46
    Service Pricing Sheet EXAMPLE #2 48
    Work Order TEMPLATE #1 51
    Work Order TEMPLATE #2 (Guitar Setup) 52
    Guitar Setup Spec Sheet EXAMPLE 53
    Business Startup Checklist 54
    Company Overview Example 55
    One Page Business Plan 56
    Press Release EXAMPLE 57
    Warranty Policy EXAMPLES 58
    Accounting Forms 59
ABOUT THE AUTHOR 61
NOTES 62

INTRODUCTION

Turning one of your passions into your job is a liberating and exciting experience. If you've been honing your guitar repair skills for a few years, you may be thinking about how life could be if you ran your own business. The good news is that you can create a successful business doing guitar repair. This guide is intended to answer any questions that you may have and perhaps even some you hadn't thought about. After learning all the ins-and-outs of this very niche business, I'm sharing it with you in hopes that it may save you some time, energy, money and frustration. If there were ever a guide when I started out, it would have been such an incredible resource to have. For myself, I had to figure it out the hard way - trial and error. I didn't have a mentor, just a strong desire to succeed using the skills I already had.

Do you need a business degree to be successful? No, but you definitely need some education, and you also need a plan. I have assembled all the relevant business information that you may want to familiarise yourself with. Reading through will point you in the right direction, keeping in mind every local, state, country has its specific laws and bylaws that the self-employed must adhere to. You will need to research this as it pertains to you and your specific situation. I've also included a section on accounting and good accounting practices because keeping track of your money is the first priority when operating a successful business.

Besides the business fundamentals, I have listed all the equipment and the tools you'll need for a startup and beyond. These are the costs you may incur with either a home-based or commercial shop. There is also a section on advertising, marketing, how to gain the customer base you need, and most importantly, how to have them keep coming back.

So go for it! Live the dream. And remember there are many out there in the world that won't have the opportunity to do so, so do it well!

I wish you all the best in starting a successful guitar repair business. Stop by my website sometime at **www.learn-guitarsetups.com** check out all the other articles and info I have made available. If you have purchased this book at an online retailer, please take a moment and submit a review - your opinion is valuable and very appreciated!

Cheers,

NOTE: The work described in this guide is intended for individuals with basic mechanical skills. If you do not understand the described procedures or are uncomfortable using tools, please leave this kind of work to a qualified technician.

GETTING STARTED

I've been 'modding' and fixing guitars as long as I've been playing them. I eventually got some real training from a world-class luthier, which lead me to work full-time in guitar repair for many years. If you live in a city similar to mine, you may have several guitar stores in the city. Retail is by far, the best training grounds for your work. There're many reasons for this. If you work in a busy store, you'll never run out of work and the work will be diverse. Setups, restringing, broken parts, replacing parts, warranty work, you name it, you'll be doing it. A good repair tech is an excellent problem solver first and foremost. Secondly, it's having experience with successful jobs, and the more, the better. You need to learn not only how temperamental wooden musical instruments can be, but also gain the exposure to many different types of guitars, all with their different problems. Another benefit to working in a store is, many times they will either have or can obtain the tools needed for the work. It's the 21st century, so use the right tool for the job at hand. And yes, there is a correct tool for just about every job you'll face.

Besides the work experience, you'll gain exposure to the work culture, customer base (very important), your fellow employees (networking, also very important) and the day-to-day running in a retail environment. It's good to learn the difference between working on a buddy's guitar in one afternoon, and then working all day, every day on an endless stack of guitars. Being hunched over a bench 8 hours a day may not be for everyone. Granted, you may find a working situation where it's not so demanding. Also, when you're working for yourself, you'll be setting your own hours.

DAY IN THE LIFE OF RUNNING A GUITAR SHOP

When you do break out on your own, what can you expect? Do you have an established customer base already or do you need to establish one? Will you be contracting out to any guitar stores? Are you starting out fresh from ground zero? Are you doing this and juggling another line of work or your music career?

In my experience, I have found that people want what they want, when they want it (which is usually yesterday). So until you have become the "messiah of guitar repair", some people will insist on convenience when getting their equipment fixed, or they go elsewhere. If you have some seriously skilled competition, this is the last thing you want to happen. What this comes down to is accommodating them by either running certain hours or operating by appointment (and being available to take appointments when *they* are available). I've tried it *all* over the years and, I can attest that it can be one of those catch-22 situations at times. Those who want to be self-employed, often want more freedom, more time and more choice in their daily life.

My most successful and personally satisfying years were when I was running a home-based repair shop by appointment. I was available every day to take appointments. I had the most personal time I've ever had, and my finances weren't in bad shape either. Although I did lose some potential customers because many people do not want to make an appointment, they just want to show up somewhere and get the service they need. I did exercise some personal boundaries with my time. Being available for appointments can put your personal time and life in the backseat. When exactly will you work and not work? How do you establish that boundary when every phone call matters? It can be done, but it will lead to lost business here and there. Or you make yourself available every day, although that can become exhausting over time. Also, you will need to be wary of some people wanting to take advantage of your time. Besides that, some people just won't take a chance with a home-based shop without a well-established reputation. Having a commercial location gives a new customer a sense of security when they are handing over their prized possession to a stranger.

If you can keep your costs of living on the lower side, and have the resources and space to do so, a home-based business may be for you. Otherwise, you'll need to consider going the commercial route.

COMMERCIAL

There may be a few ways in how you approach the commercial route. Early on, I had a rehearsal studio, so I started offering guitar repair as well. Makes sense, right? Maybe there's a new startup out there like a music studio or school that you could rent space in. That would absolutely be the way to start out if at all possible. Built-in traffic, cheap rent, and so much more networking opportunities. You won't be alone, and that's a good thing, especially in this industry.

Perhaps you can strike up a deal with a local studio or even a store that doesn't offer repairs so that there is a business for your customers to go to and drop off/pick up their gear.

With a little creativity, there're many ways to go about setting up your business. What's important is that it works for you *and* your customers. Anything less won't last the long term.

Other options are alternative rental spaces. If you looked into retail space, you might find it's the most expensive to rent. But what about office space or even better, warehouse space (which may be the most cost effective)? The location is important, but if you do not have plans to go full retail and just stick with repair and parts, people will come to you (as long as it's worth the trip).

There's no need to spend your time hunting down the perfect space, have a commercial real estate agent do it for you. You don't need to be concerned with the cost or getting a bill because they take a cut of the deal, which is how many real estate transactions work. They can also negotiate on your behalf. You'd be surprised how many places aren't even listed publicly. I found my first commercial sub-let space through an agent, and it was everything I could have hoped for.

I found as soon as I opened a commercial location my business instantly increased. I didn't advertise for it or create any public awareness outside of my customer base. Can you guess the reason why?

It comes down to ease of access and regular business hours. I can't tell you how great it was to work business hours in the sense that I didn't need to juggle customer appointments any longer. It was nice to have clear, established boundaries when I was open for business and when I wasn't. It was also really nice to go home at the end of the day without any reminders of repair work staring at me in the face. Of course, this all came with a cost of having less personal time than what I was used to, and I was working harder, longer hours since I more than doubled my overhead from the previous home-based shop.

Eventually, I incorporated retail, for example, used equipment alongside accessories and parts. So people would come in just to check out what was new. Foot traffic increased as well as local awareness. Other stores were pointing me out to their customers, and business was good.

Business cycles
I don't know if you've ever witnessed this, but many businesses have cycles that seem to ebb and flow. You may have noticed it sometimes when everyone seems to go into the store at the same time, then seemingly all leave at the same time. It's a strange phenomenon as you're witnessing it, but something to be aware of as an aspect of life when self-employed. What does this mean for you when starting out? Well, you may have ten guitars come in on Monday and nothing again until Saturday. While this might worry you, and rightfully so, it can be the ebb and flow of guitar

repair in a small shop or town. Later on, I will show you how to set up your break-evens and determine how much business you actually need on a weekly and monthly basis.

Another aspect to consider is the low rate of return business, even from your loyal customer base. In fact, new customers are what will keep your business going. It is the shortcoming of any service business. If you think about it, a great job well done will not necessarily yield more business from that same client, unless of course, your customer has more instruments that require repair of some sort. It's not like being a hairdresser, where you will see that customer again in 3-5 weeks. This is where specialising and incorporating retail comes in. If you want to be the destination for guitar repair, consider being the destination for parts, or cool used gear. For these reasons, you may want to consider what other ways you can create income streams within your business.

WHAT IS IT ACTUALLY LIKE?

Guitar repair can be a lot of fun, full of challenges and problems to solve. If you love gear, you'll get to check out more than your fair share of it. No two days are alike, and no two guitars are exactly the same. You've really got to love tinkering, fixing and solving problems creatively.

Guitar repair, as a business, is usually a service that is billed out to the customer in hourly segments, similar to an automotive mechanic. With that said, it can become quite taxing if you must produce a lot of turn-over every day (just like anything). I'd recommend for anybody, to keep the workload low to avoid potential burnout, if at all possible. Or, if you can help it, make repairs a part of your daily responsibilities, instead of the entirety of it. Besides that, it's an enjoyable work, relatively relaxing and low stress. Customers are generally grateful and loyal.

SPECIALIZING, FINDING YOUR NICHE

I can't say what sort of competition you may have, but for myself, it has always been retail stores who offered repair services. I worked for a handful of them, so I knew where they fell short, and I knew that I could offer more. For example, even though there was a handful of stores around the city (which comes down to a lot of choices for people), they didn't necessarily hire the most skilled help. So then I'm sure you guess one of my niches.

Right out of the gate, it was to do outstanding, highly detailed professional level work and (hopefully) change the playing field in the process. This intention gave me a mission to do superior work, as well as the drive to educate customers about how their instruments work and should be maintained. I have a diverse and unique background, so I embraced all my prior experience, and this became my niche'. Besides offering a refined skill set, I've always been into 'modding' guitars. So I offered major custom work, and I got the most interesting jobs, let me tell you. I rarely, if ever, refused a job, no matter how ridicules a request. It kept life interesting while paying the bills. Additionally, I have a book out on assembling guitar kits called "How to Build & Setup Guitar Kits like a Pro: An Easy Guide for Bolt-on Necks". I wrote this to be included in a series following my first book "How to Setup Your Guitar like a Pro: An Easy Guide for Beginners". The aforementioned is one of my other niches, as I've built numerous guitars from kits, the first ones being my own, and over the years I have refined efficient methods and configurations while using the parts provided by my customers. A lot of the time, the parts did not fit together, and I had to modify what I had to work with. Little did those customers know just how much work that actually took in those times.

The next page shows an example of my **service sheet** for you to use as a reference. It was refined over five years and broken down into several specific jobs for numerous reasons. The first reason is that you need a compass when charging for your work. Do you know how long the job is going to take? Every time? Experience will tell you this, and until you have that experience you will need to follow a guideline, and stick with it. We will talk more about **pricing your services** in a later chapter. If you were to compare being a guitar tech with being a mechanic, there are some similarities. This is one way you can approach your pricing. You can have a shop rate, with common jobs at a flat rate, based on your hourly rate (for the most part). It's important to consider that some jobs may take longer than quoted. Sometimes you eat that extra time. When you are starting out, you'll eat all of it (if you plan on running a respectful business that is). There is no excuse, other than lack of experience, for going over the time quoted. What actually happens, is the more experience you have, the quicker and more efficient you become. Sometimes, the customer should be notified when the costs will be higher. For example, when it resulted based solely on the instrument's condition and was not noticed earlier.

Service Sheet Example #1 with optional add-ons

Restring/clean

- Add strap button (acoustic)
- Dowel/drill strap button (stripped)
- Tuner install

Setups (restring, clean, check hardware/ electronics, adjust truss, bridge, saddles, nut, p/ups, intonation)
Optimized/add-ons
- Extra dirty guitar/stickers removed
- High frets seated & glued
- Fret-ends filed/dressed
- Frets re-beveled and dressed (smooth, easy feel)
- Fret level (light/optimise low action)
- Fret level (deep, bad frets, neck)
- Dlx. fret buff (all scratches out, polished sheen/smooth playing)
- Block tremolo one side
- Block tremolo both sides

Electronics
- Clean/test
- Install new part (pot, switch, etc.)
- Install complete set of controls
- Fix solder joint(s)
- Rewire a muck-up
- Modify guitar for custom controls (route, drill, etc.)

Pickups
- Potting/re-potting
- Install new electric p/up
- Install new acoustic soundhole p/up with endpin jack
- Install new acoustic under saddle p/up (req . setup)

Hot Rodding/upgrading

- Nut (Bone/Tusq, etc.)
- Earvana compensated nut (improves intonation)
- Buzz Feiten compensated nut retrofit (improves intonation)
- New saddle (acoustic)
- New saddle (acoustic- compensated)
- Upgrade pickups
- Upgrade hardware
- Upgrade electronics and controls
- Pickup dipping (helps eliminate microphonic feedback)

Tele upgrades/add-ons
- Drill down & wax bridge (prevent feedback)
- Feedback control (drill down & wax bridge, extra padding at bridge pickup)
- Add new saddles/compensated
- Reverse control plate
- 4-way switch

"Import" guitar problems
- Dlx. fret polish, seat/glue and level frets
- Upgrade electronics
- Upgrade hardware

Custom Services
- Custom modifications
- Custom routing (pickups, bridges, etc.)
- Pickguard shaping
- Building and assembly

So with a service sheet, you have your general costs laid out, and it's easy to communicate with the customer. Even they can read it. I broke mine down into an ala-carte' style list with "add-on services". I found this worked well for my particular situation, mostly in communication. They come in for a setup, but say, also need a new jack. It's easy to add-on the additional costs, and there will be less chance of doing work you don't end up billing for. It may seem petty to some people, but this is the name of the business game, and how a serious shop operates. Everything should be billed out, just like any legit service business. Every dime helps **you make a profit**, which will be discussed more in a later chapter.

Another reason for having a service sheet is that you can print them off and leave them with your customers' guitar. They go home and open the case and have all your contact information as well as a drooling list of possibilities they can dream about undertaking with their guitar, or their other guitar(s), or buddy's guitar....you get the idea. This idea works well. If you look at mine, it almost makes suggestions on all the possibilities of improvements or customizations that a person can make. Couple that with a price list of popular pickups or parts you sell and you'll have a winning combination.

YOUR TRAINING & EXPERIENCE

Your biggest asset is your training and experience level. It's attractive to gain a few skills and want to run out and start fixing people's guitars. I've seen this time and time again and ultimately it never works out very well for them, but it does for the guy/gal down the street, who has more experience/ skill under their belt, (like yours truly). Even though it has kept me quite busy fixing other's mistakes and gaining their customer base, I shake my head every time, because it doesn't do the industry any good by prematurely setting out to take over the world. Thankfully with the rise of Youtube and other websites, people are becoming more educated in maintenance and luthiery globally, and this is a good thing.

There are some world-class luthier schools out there, and for some, this may be a good choice. Building guitars will help you fix them, but don't confuse the two being the same. I've met builders that have no business in guitar repair. They are completely different skill sets but truly complement each other as well as you can imagine. Many aspects of guitar building will help in the world of repair including learning finishing technique, proper tool use, understanding and working with wood while exercising highly detailed work, among other things.

Ultimately, the best training is working under an accomplished guitar tech. In other trades, a person would follow an apprenticeship until they have several years of training. Approach guitar repair in a similar manner. Nothing can be a substitution for years of experience and knowledge, and the truth of it is, there is no end to the learning.

Another aspect I see with people jumping in before they are ready is in underestimating the need to be a good guitar *player*. Why would this matter when you're just tweaking them, right? Well, I'm sure most technical repair methods can be taught to and employed by anyone who is able and willing. But if it is simply a mechanical procedure, there is a personal touch that will be missing, and I can't stress enough that the most successful and revered techs have that personal touch. In this day in age, where craft and personal touch is lacking in so many areas of society, it is a highly valuable trait to offer. If your customers are better guitar players than you, will you confidently understand what they need from their guitar?

Here is a partial list of some notable schools

Summit School of Guitar Building and Repair
www.luthiers-international.com/

Galloup School of Guitar Building and Professional Guitar Repair
www.galloupguitars.com/school.htm

American School of Lutherie
http://www.americanschooloflutherie.com/

Benedetto Guitars
http://www.benedettoguitars.com/

Chicago School of Guitar Making
http://www.specimenproducts.com/chicago-school-of-guitar-making/

O'Brien Guitars
http://www.obrienguitars.com/

Timeless Instruments
http://www.timelessinstruments.com/

THE BUSINESS & HOW TO PROFIT

To put it simply, the nature of this business is in charging a predetermined amount of money for a service you provide. Seems straight forward enough, right? If you have plans of doing this business full-time, I should make you aware that your time may be much more difficult to juggle. Since doing the repair work is *how* you earn money, you will also need to account for the time needed for advertising, social networking, emailing, answer telephone calls, dealing with suppliers and interacting with customers, that of which can go on and on, easily occupying an entire day. With that being said, you may want to budget your service hours. How many billable hours can you actually work in a day, every day? Out of that budget, how many of those hours will not be billable due to unforeseen circumstances or other problems? What if you get held up on the job for 1 or 2 hours more than you had planned? Add in customer interactions, etc., and you may quickly come to the conclusion that you need a clone of yourself to do everything! Time management is the trickiest aspect when starting a new business. It seems as though there's never enough time to get everything done.

HOW MUCH TO CHARGE
When it comes down to charging for your services, you will quickly see why being diligent with your billing will either make or break you. Decide what your services are worth and bill accordingly. Checking with the market rate for your experience level, your competitions' rates, and your financial needs, you should be able to come to a conclusion on what your hourly rate you can charge. Keeping in mind, if people aren't willing to pay your rate, you may be way out to lunch. It's got to be reasonable for what you offer, and you should feel comfortable asking that amount when face-to-face with a new customer.

Example:

Local Shop 1: $55/hr
Local Shop 2: $60/hr
Local Shop 3: $60/hr
Local Shop 4: $75/hr

With these examples, you also need to determine what they offer for that shop rate. How is their reputation? Are the techs skilled or unskilled? Do they do the bare minimum or exceed expectations? Do they have a guarantee? And so on.

If those shops are on par with what you can offer, I would find the average and consider asking $60/hr. If you still have a lot to learn, I would charge less. The amount you charge depends on your experience/knowledge level and the local market rate. In trades, the Journeyman may make $30-$50/hr, but the apprentice may make $15-$18/hr. Keep this in mind and respect those that have gone before you in establishing a decent market-rate.

It's not a bad idea to charge a little less while you build your customer base up, and slowly raise it up to the local market rate over time. You'll get more customers who will want to take advantage of the lower costs, which in turn will help establish your business. If your experience and skills far exceed the competition, charge for it and set yourself part (and be prepared to prove yourself).

Once you've got that decided, figure out how many hours you can bill out every day, in the span of a week. Let's say 5 hours within an 8 hour period, which is a realistic workload amount in a busy shop. In a workweek of, let's say, five days, that would amount to 25 billable hours or 100 in a perfect month.

So, granted you have 5 hours of work every day, and you bill out those 5 hours successfully, in a month's time you'll have a nice little profit. Let's apply some basic math. For the sake of explanation, we'll say your rate is $35/hour, so you'll net $3500 in a successful month of 100 billed hours. From this total, you must subtract all your operating costs to get your total gross profit.

BREAK-EVEN AMOUNTS
A break-even total is the minimal amount of money you need every month to get by. To determine this, tally up all your operating costs, including your personal costs. A typical break-even formula usually suggests including your salary (or the salary you want to pay yourself), but with this kind of startup, you'll be taking every dollar you can muster up at first. So I'll suggest just your personal costs include your living costs, like rent, groceries, etc. (assuming a basic, sole proprietorship start-up).

Once you have this total, divide it by the number of weeks in the month, and you have your break-even amount established for each week and the month. Having a determined break-even amount will help you establish a budget for your service hours. You will also know every day where your business stands.

Break-even example
Operating costs:
Rent $1000
Utilities $200
Internet/Phone $75
Insurance $75
Advertising $300
Personal Costs $1500
Total $3150

Minus estimated monthly revenues $3500

Gross profit $350. Which leads us into the next section.

Additional Revenue Streams

As mentioned previously, if you can supplement your repairs with another revenue stream you will have more cash flow, enabling you to ride out the typical ups and downs with less stress. There are plenty of complimenting ventures you can research. Some examples are selling replacement parts, specialising in supplies your competition doesn't carry, selling pre-made electronic upgrade kits, building or selling guitar kits, selling used gear, offering consignment sales, or even being a dealer yourself for some great, sought-after guitar gear. Other ideas to explore could be in music lessons, rockband-style group lessons, guitar your own guitars for sale and/ or workshops.

When it comes to dealing in guitar parts, I found it beneficial to have the brands asked for but to 'upsell' the niche brands that I specialised in. If you can offer expertise in parts and provide better options than a big brand store, you'll gain a receptive community of customers interested in what you have to sell. My particular branding was more of a custom build shop, so I stocked higher end parts and everything no else would. I took pride in having some great lines that no one else in town had. Even though I couldn't price some things as low as the big box guys, customers still ordered and purchased through me, the little guy. By the way, there are many who would rather.

Special ordering is your secret weapon when you don't have the purchasing power of a small bank. In this business, your customers are accustom to waiting, and with some things, they don't mind a couple of weeks ordering time. There will always be those who will go and order things for themselves off eBay, but remember as a dealer you will always have the upper hand in retail. For example, you can offer warranty and service, where online sellers *usually* do not.

When it comes to choosing your product lines, research your competition. See what they sell, and look at where they fall short. Finding and filling a need is a sure-fire way to find success amid thick competition.

Dealerships / Wholesale accounts
When buying products for resale, you want to approach a wholesale company first. A wholesaler is an intermediary entity in the distribution channel that buys in bulk and sells to resellers rather than to consumers. There are some relatively well-known guitar parts suppliers based in the U.S. who will be happy to set you up with a wholesale account. All you need is a copy of your business license to set it up. The big notorious two are:

Allparts - www.allparts.com
Allparts is the world's largest distributor of guitar, bass, and amplifier parts, having official international distributors on six continents to meet the world's need for quality guitar parts to make quality music (50% discount off retail).

WD Music - www.wdbiz.com
Founded in 1978, WD Music Products has grown into one of the world's largest suppliers of stringed instrument parts. (50% discount off retail).

There are other online retailers and some manufacturers that offer a wholesale program, which is usually just a discount off retail when buying multiples of one item. I wouldn't suggest going this route as you won't likely be getting a true wholesale cost- which is what you need as a retailer, and without that, your competitors will gain the edge in their pricing strategies. There are times you may choose to go through these businesses. Perhaps you can't get the brands elsewhere or otherwise are out of stock from your usual supplier. Here are a couple of noteworthy companies to check out.

Mojotone - www.mojotone.com

Mojotone is a manufacturer of amplifier cabinet, amp kits, pickups and much more. A wholesale account will save you almost enough to make some profit when reselling their great gear (30% off retail, at the time of writing) when compared to their online pricing that is. They also sell some notable brands.

CE Distribution - www.cedist.com
Although claiming they are a distributor, I have noticed with some items that the costs are just as high as retail, so I will label them more a mixed supplier. They do have some tools, speakers, tubes and some cool gadgets. Mixed discounts.

Traditional Distributors
Traditional distributors buy noncompeting products or product lines, warehouses them, and resells them to retailers (or direct to the end users or customers). Most distributors provide strong manpower and cash support to the supplier or manufacturer's promotional efforts. These would include the companies who distribute all those guitars and accessory lines like Ernie Ball or D'Addario. If you want to get hooked up with the big guys, all you need is a business license and some cash flow to make your purchases (many of them expect this on a regular basis to some degree or another). I recommend waiting on approaching them until you have a storefront (often required) and substantial cash flow for the initial stocking order. It's easy to research these companies, simply look up the brands you're interested in and send them an email.

A note on wholesale clubs or programs. You may come across some wholesale 'club' or program, I've run into a few. I don't know too much about them as I have always steered clear. Don't ever sign up with a company that requires a subscription service or annual fee. True wholesalers want your business and don't have any reason to charge you for access to their product lines. They make money by selling products to their dealer network, just like you make money by selling to your customers.

Boutique Manufacturers
These days there are many boutique pickup builders and parts manufacturers out there and could be the competitive edge you are looking for. Some of them will only build to order, and this aspect won't necessarily appeal to big box retailers. Besides, a lot of this stuff is high-end and worlds apart from the mainstream. There's far too many to list but here's a few to check out:

Lindy Fralin Pickups - http://www.fralinpickups.com/
Fralin Pickups have long been at the top of the list for aftermarket pickups, arguably the most impactful change you can make to an electric guitar

Bareknuckle Pickups - https://bareknucklepickups.co.uk
Bare Knuckle Pickups is a privately owned business based in the South West of England, UK, specialising in hand-wound electric guitar pickups.

Lollar Pickups - http://www.lollarguitars.com/
For more than a decade, Jason Lollar has designed and built some of the most sought-after pickups for electric guitar, bass and steel guitar.

The Creamery - http://www.creamery-pickups.co.uk/
Custom Guitars, Custom Made Handwound Pickups - Made in Manchester

Emerson Custom - http://www.emersoncustom.com/
Emerson Custom is a small, family-owned American company located in Tulsa, Oklahoma USA founded in 2009, offering hand-built and wired guitar effects pedals, prewired assemblies, and quality guitar components/parts.

RS Guitarworks - https://store.rsguitarworks.net/

RS Guitarworks builds custom-designed, handcrafted guitars, legendary electronic upgrades, aged parts, or restoration services.

MARKUPS, MAPS, and YOUR COMPETITIVE EDGE

MARKUP
A markup is a retail term used to explain the percentage or amount an item is priced above its cost. In guitar stores, you will usually have items priced between 30-50% above cost, depending on the price range, item, local competition and business plan. For example, a guitar tuner may be priced 50% above cost, whereas a guitar may be priced just 30% or slightly less, depending on its price range.

MAP
MAP stands for *Minimum Advertised Price*, meaning, any item you sell that has a MAP, must not be advertised for a lower cost. You have agreed with the wholesaler you will not advertise the price under MAP and in doing so may revoke your dealership.

Why do MAP agreements exist?

- To promote fair competition across all distribution channels
- To maintain brand identity and value
- To allow smaller sellers to compete with larger retailers
- To prevent under pricing
- To protect seller margins

Although MAP agreements exist to protect seller margins, the price isn't the only concern. Brand value retention is also a factor to retailers and manufacturers alike.

MSRP
MSRP stands for *Manufacturer's Suggested Retail Price*, and as it states, is simply a suggestion.

UNDERCUTTING
Those who are new to business may be so eager to make money that they enter the market without a pricing strategy. It may seem like a great idea to simply price below your competitions'. If you are running a brick-and-mortar business, a good practice is having a 30% or higher markup. This minimum markup will allow some room for bartering/negotiating and sale pricing or other promotional strategies, while still making some profit. Online sellers have notoriously priced much lower than this, and now this has become the norm for much e-commerce.

INCREASING YOUR STREET CREDIBILITY

If your intentions are to set yourself apart from your competition, there are a few different ways you can increase your perceived value in the marketplace. This niche' ties into your marketing strategies, but I'll offer a few examples so that you can see how.

Working under a well-known luthier or tech.
This can be tied into your sales copy or pitch and will give you a little bump in the clout department. You'll want to be able to live up to that individual's name, so be well practised before making those claims.

Working for a manufacturer.
Not unlike the aforementioned, working for Gibson or Fender looks pretty impressive to anyone wanting their guitars looked after by a professional.

Accreditation.
Let's face it, you probably wouldn't see a professional if they didn't have proper accreditation. Taking courses that offer Certification in your field of work always gives off a sense of professionalism and also helps fill up the walls with a Certificate or two.

Additional training.
There are a few ways to get some speciality training which can expand your service offering. One of the more notorious speciality's is becoming an **Authorized Buzz Feiten Retrofitter** (www.buzzfeiten.com). The Buzz Feiten tuning system consists of installing their proprietary shelf nut to a very precise location and applying specific pitch offsets for tempered tuning. The training is available in 2 tiers. The first, as a correspondence dealer package that includes video training and supplies, aimed at electric guitar. The second requires hands-on training from an Authorized Buzz Feiten Training Facility. This speciality comes with some substantial costs and may or may not be worthwhile for your potential customer base. **Galloup School of Guitar Building** (www.galloupguitars.com) offers some speciality workshops including pickup winding and tube amp building, as well as many other programs worth checking out.

Warranty Service
If you have a commercial space, you may qualify to be a warranty depot for major guitar brands such as Fender Musical Instruments, Martin or Taylor Guitars. This is a good way to gain more customers and simultaneously gives your customers an impression of professionalism and proven skill. Often these companies will scrutinise who their authorised service centres are, and some may even offer training, such as with Taylor Guitars. Taylor offers a broad network of service centres for their customers, broken down into service levels Bronze, Silver and Gold. Each can offer a specific capacity of repair work on a warranty basis. Fender has a similar system although without any specific factory training.

Doing warranty work will as mentioned, increase your presence substantially. The reality of it is, many more phone calls and inquiries, both warranty and non-warranty issues. When doing any warranty work, you make an agreement with the manufacturer to uphold their processes and procedures, and in turn, they will pay you a pre-determined rate for the job at hand. It may or may not mirror your shop rates (they're often lower), and comes with more paperwork than you may be accustom to doing. Once the job is complete, the required paperwork must be filled out and then submitted to the factory Service Manager, who will, in turn, initiate the accounting so that you can get paid. Because of the long, drawn out process, consider this an additional revenue stream over your main bread and butter.

Being listed as an Installer or Dealer for notorious after-market brands
Another way to help build your reputation is to gain some industry referrals from manufacturers such as **Evertune**, **Earvana**, **Hipshot**, etc. You may need to have experience installing their products, but most often this only takes an email to be listed on their website. When it comes to

after-market parts, many brands will open a dealership without a major stocking requirement (this is where you are required to stock X amount of products to be open as their Dealer). When one of their customers is looking for an Installer or Dealer in their area, your contact information comes up, and you have an opportunity to earn their business.

SETTING UP SHOP: A Simple Process to Getting You Started

Break down large goals into small tasks
Depending on your self-employment intentions, you may begin feeling overwhelmed with all the start-up tasks presenting themselves. My suggestion is to get out a notebook and pen and start breaking down all the things you need to do. Big ideas need to be broken down into small, manageable tasks so that you can begin chipping away at them in an efficient manner. This is a practice and skill that any entrepreneur will tell you, and as you carry on your business, you will be doing this on a daily basis, to some degree or another. As an example, write the task at the top of a page and in point blank, list off every step that needs to be done for that goal to come to fruition. You'll notice in doing this, that more tasks may come up along the way that you didn't originally consider or think of, and realistically, this is the nature of tackling big goals. Chipping away, one task at a time will eventually accomplish your goals. See the **RESOURCES** section in the back of the book for a **Business Startup Checklist** to point you in the right direction.

Make your plan and stick to it.
It may seem obvious, but when things get rockin', all sorts of deviations from your business focus can come up along the way. This would be one reason to write a business plan if you indeed have a plan for your business. Keep in mind, if you don't know where you're going, you'll never get there.

Write a one-page business plan.
At this stage, there isn't any reason to make a robust business plan unless you are seeking investment or financing. So to get started, create your own simple, one-page business plan that is an overview of your business idea. This should include:

- Your vision: What will be the end result of your startup? How will it all look?
- Your mission statement: Explain the reason your business exists to serve the public.
- Your objectives: What are your goals? What will lead to the accomplishment of your mission and your vision?
- Your basic strategies: How are you going to achieve the objectives you just listed?
- A simple plan of action: List out the tasks required to achieve your stated objectives.

Figure out your cash flow and budgets.
Typically, guitar repair is a micro-business, and not requiring large amounts of capital. For many, this is one of the most appealing qualities when starting this type of business. With that being said, there is still the need to determine all your start-up costs and attribute another 20% to incidentals while operating. It's also important to figure out how long you can stay in business before turning a profit.

You should plan and set up your business with profitability in mind for the first 30 to 90 days, but having a budget reserve so you can survive if things go leaner than expected.

Decide on a business structure / legal entity.
Many of those who get into guitar repair (or any other new businesses) will keep life simple and operate as a sole proprietor. A sole proprietorship in most cases doesn't require filing much legal paperwork (if any in some cases), and therefore keeps day-to-day accounting concerns relatively easy. Anything other will require more paperwork and probably a trip or two to the lawyer's office. Also keep in mind that as business becomes more established, you can decide at any time to change the legal structure as you see fit. Your business structure matters the most at tax time, as it

is *how* your tax authority will identify your business. An accountant will share all the ins-and-outs when setting up your business in one way or another. They can lay everything out on the table so that it makes the most sense. There is also a lot of free information available online as well. The next chapter will describe **BUSINESS STRUCTURES** in more detail.

Take care of your money.
Whatever you decide on, keep your business banking separate from your personal bank accounts from the beginning. It will only get unnecessarily confusing at tax time to try and distinguish which transactions are from business and which from personal. You are essentially lightening your workload just by doing so. Otherwise, every month you will need to go through your banking records and highlight which transactions are business transactions, relating to your expenditures and revenues (a headache!). Why would you do this? All income must be accounted for at tax time, and every cost that you can identify (with receipt) will offset your revenue amount, and thereby lowering your tax owing, although not equally (the chips are stacked in your tax authority's favour). Many banks offer free business accounts now, so signup with one of them to help keep your overhead as low as possible.

To setup a business bank account, you'll need your DBA (doing business as) or corporate filing paperwork and an initial deposit, as required by most financial institutions.

Setup a website.
A website should be a no-brainer. A large percentage of your new customers will likely find you by searching "guitar repair" in their Google or equivalent search engine. If you don't have any experience with websites, there are plenty of websites that offer an easy, drag-and-drop style web building interface, such as Wix.com or Weebly.com (*current as of the publishing date*). You will want to include some sales copy - a.k.a. your sales pitch, on the home page. You will also want to include an About Me, Services Offered, Location, and Contact Page, as a bare minimum. If you include photos and/or videos of your work, all the better. Whatever you do, do not under-estimate the importance of how good your website should look. Don't spend an hour on it and call it done. Who doesn't want to see the kind of work being offered firsthand? Invest in a great site, full of information and you will reap the benefits. One of them is having common questions answered for you, including services offered and hours of operation, etc.

Advertise & open for business.
Be realistic in your expectations when you are officially "open for business". If you have a customer base, great, otherwise learn to hustle.

You can drive traffic to your website by sharing it with all your friends and family, and then asking them to share it with all *their* friends and family. All those hits will help index your website by the search engine. Next, you will want people to find it through other websites, like Facebook for example. You can set up a simple Facebook Ad or a simple Google AdWords account with a budget cap. More details about these ads can be found in the **ADVERTISING** section.

BUSINESS PLANS

A standard business plan is a document describes what you plan to do and how you plan to do it. A one-page business plan will often suffice for many micro-start-ups. For a larger endeavour, including any partnerships or financing, a business plan will be necessary. I will highlight what a typical business plan consists of, but since it is a rather dull subject for most, will keep this chapter short. There is an abundance of templates, how-to articles and more online.

A typical business plan includes some or all of the following:

- Mission statement and/or vision statement to articulate what you're trying to create;
- Description of your company and product or service;
- Description of how your product or service is different;
- Market analysis that discusses the market you're trying to enter, competitors, where you fit, and what type of market share you believe you can secure;
- Description of your management team, including the experience of key team members and previous successes;
- How you plan to market the product or service;
- Analysis of your company's strengths, weaknesses, opportunities, and threat, which will show that you're realistic and have considered opportunities and challenges;
- Develop a cash flow statement, so you understand what your needs are now and will be in the future (a cash flow statement also can help you consider how cash flow could impact growth);
- Revenue projections; and
- Summary/conclusion that wraps everything together (this also could be an executive summary at the beginning of the plan).

You can keep it simple and just make it for your own benefit, and pass on the irrelevant topics. Even a micro businesses will benefit from a simple business plan. For example, it will help you break down all your costs of business, including a detailed list of your startup costs. Cash flow is often an issue with new startups, so the more costs you can identify ahead of time, the better. Additionally, a business plan will help identify your competition and highlight their weakness and strengths. Sometimes going through the motions of writing it all out helps solidify what you can offer to the marketplace. It will also help you identify your weakness and strengths. Furthermore, it will aid in developing a strategy, avoiding short-sighted mistakes, and provide detailed analysis for those pursuing funding from banks or investors.

BUSINESS STRUCTURES

With any business startup, you need to decide on the structure of the business. The reason for this is to identify your business to the tax authorities, which will govern how you will be taxed. Will you keep it simple as a Sole Proprietorship, go into a Partnership with another, or file as a Corporation? Your day-to-day activities may remain similar within any of these business structures, but your accounting and taxes will differ significantly. There are some pros and cons to consider.

SOLE PROPRIETORSHIP

A sole proprietorship is the simplest legal structure but has some drawbacks. This kind of business is the easiest to start because you only need to obtain the licenses required to begin business operation. This will require a little research on your part, as every city, state and country may differ. Often there is a business license that is required, as issued by the city and/or state. You may also be required to register your fictitious business name as a "Doing Business As", also known as DBA, with your local or federal municipalities. Apparently, there are a few states in the USA that do not require the registering of fictitious business names. Even when it is required, many businesses do not bother to register their fictitious name. Some people will simply use their legal name, for example, "Joe Smith Guitar Repair".

More often a small business owner will choose to start as a sole proprietorship, and as the business grows, explores other options.

Income and Taxation

The sole proprietor's income from the business is treated as personal income. In Canada and the U.S., you can declare this Income and Loss from a Business or Profession, on a standard individual income tax return. The simplicity makes tax time a breeze, at least when comparing to the other business structures. You won't necessarily need an accountant, and that's a big cost you're saving. The trick is to keep your records organised. I have included some accounting forms at the back of this book to help you. Furthermore, these and other forms are available as a free download at *www.learn-guitarsetups.com/grb-downloads.*

On the topic of taxation, it's a smart idea to put away 20-25% of your revenues every month so that when it comes time to pay, you actually have the money to pay. Taxes can really add up over a year, and without savings, it can put your new business in a bad crunch right off the bat.

What Are the Advantages of a Sole Proprietorship?
- You keep it simple & manageable.
- You are in business quickly and easily.
- There are hardly any restrictions and very few forms to fill out.
- As a sole proprietor, you control all of the money made by the business.
- You make all business operation calls.
- You are management and, thus, can respond more quickly to day-to-day changes and decisions.
- You experience less government control and taxation. You don't have to keep incorporation records and annual corporate records.
- You don't have to do a separate tax return for the business, and you don't have to prepare a balance sheet for the business.

What Are the Disadvantages of a Sole Proprietorship?
- As a sole proprietor, you are responsible for 100 percent of all business debts and obligations, as well as any other legal obligations. This liability covers all of the proprietor's assets, including his or her house and car. Additional insurance coverage may

be needed to cover personal injury or physical loss that may hamper the continuity of the business.
- The death, physical impairment, or mental incapacitation of the owner can result in the termination of the business.
- Difficulty raising capital or arranging long-term financing (based on proprietors assets).
- All the decision-making power rests with one individual.
- A sole proprietorship appears less professional than a corporation or an LLC.
- Income tax will be based on your business's revenues, as well as any other income revenues you may have and could be quite high.

PARTNERSHIPS

A Partnership is a legal association of two or more persons carrying on business. Although not required by law, you may have to create Articles of Partnership. For instance, if you want to open a company bank account, they may require these papers. These articles would define the contributions made by the partners to the business—financial, managerial, material, or other. They would also define the roles of each partner in the business relationship. All articles should be filed with your secretary of state.

Partnership Agreements

It is important to designate who is going to contribute to the partnership, and in what ways. For example, who is going to get paid and how much, and which expenses will be paid. Other details to consider are, what happens if one partner wants to terminate the partnership, which duties are specifically intended to be performed by each partner, and even approximately how much each partner is expected to work for the partnership each week. Even if your business partner is your best friend or your spouse, a good agreement can keep you all good friends.

What Are the Advantages of a Partnership?
- Setup expenses are minimal, and the legal documentation more straightforward than an incorporation.
- Partners have more motivation, as they directly share in the profits.
- It may be easier to attract capital than for a sole proprietorship.
- It is easier to execute decisions than it would be in a corporation, but it more difficult than a sole proprietorship.
- More freedom from federal regulations and taxation.

What Are the Disadvantages of a Partnership?
- Until you form a special partnership that limits the liability of one or more partners, all partners are responsible for 100 percent of the company's debts. All partners can be held liable for partnership business activities and the commitments of any partner.
- Long-term capital may be difficult to find. However, using partnership assets as collateral makes it somewhat easier than in the case of a sole proprietorship.
- If any one partner decides to quit or passes on, the partnership is dissolved. The business can still operate based on the right of survivorship and the creation of a new partnership. Partnership insurance should be considered.

INCORPORATION

Most business owners form corporations to protect themselves against financial and legal liabilities. In other words, a corporation legally keeps your business dealings, assets, and bank accounts separate from you and your assets. There are much more costs associated with filing initial paperwork when incorporating a business, often amounting to the thousands of dollars.

What Are the Advantages of a Corporation?

- **Separate liabilities:** A corporation is an entirely separate legal entity from its owners and shareholders. That means that in situations such as the company being sued or the corporation owing debts, the owners and shareholders cannot be sued or held personally liable for the debts *(although not as a hard-and-fast rule. Check your local laws regarding this)*.
- **Investors:** If you're trying to raise capital by selling shares in the company, you'll need to be incorporated. You'll also need to form a corporation if you ever plan to go public.
- **Taxes:** Depending on the corporate structure under which you choose to do business, you can elect to have pass-through taxation to your personal taxes, or you can avoid double taxation. Tax laws typically favour corporations.
- **Never-ending business:** A corporation remains a corporation even if the owner leaves, dies, or sells off the company.
- **Credibility:** A business with an Inc. or LLC extension after its name often sounds more credible to outsiders. Being incorporated can also help protect your business name in the state in which you do business.

What Are the Advantages of a Corporation?

- **Money:** As mentioned, it's not cheap to incorporate. If you're just starting out and cash flow is an issue, be prepared to pay for such costs as state filing fees, attorney fees, and other government fees.
- **More paperwork:** As a corporation, you're required to file Articles of Incorporation, bylaws, corporate minutes, certificates of good standing, and other paperwork on a regular basis.
- **More taxes to file:** You'll need to file a separate tax form and can't claim any personal tax credits on it. Plus, business losses can only be applied to the business — they can't help you on your personal taxes.

As far as advantages to incorporating, most businesses will choose one form of incorporation solely to protect the business owner and/or stockholders from personal liability for the business's debts or actions. Each structure has its individual advantages and disadvantages based on its taxation rules, organisation, and administrative overhead.

BUSINESS STARTUP CHECKLISTS (Canada, USA)

You can read up on all this fun stuff here Canada:
Canada Revenue Agency: Checklist for new small businesses
http://www.cra-arc.gc.ca/tx/bsnss/sm/chcklst-eng.html

or here if you live in the USA:
IRS: Checklist for Starting a Business
https://www.irs.gov/businesses/small-businesses-self-employed/checklist-for-starting-a-business

If you are reading from another country, search your country's taxation body (if applicable).

TYPICAL STARTUP BUSINESS COSTS

Costs, costs, costs. When starting a new business, there are so many costs that seem to come out of nowhere. There are the typical ones like your tools, computer, signage, rent, utility hookups, etc., etc. But the ones you didn't think of can leave you scrambling.

Here's a partial list of typical startup costs. Some may apply, while others do not. The more research you do, the more you can be prepared for it all.

Tools & Equipment- This goes without saying. Your tools will be one of the most expensive costs in your business. See the **TOOLS & EQUIPMENT LIST** at the back of the book for an example of your most basic tools. Shopping around for the best price is the fun part.

Business licenses and permits - Research the extent of your business license costs. In my locality, this included a business development fee that I wasn't expecting, basically doubling my expected costs from $250 to $500 (annually).

Commercial Development - Is the commercial space up to municipality standards? Will an inspection cost money? Any upgrades or improvements that need to be carried out will need to be budgeted for.

Business Filing Fees – Fictitious name statement, and reseller license fees (if applicable). Depending on where you live, these fees may be paid annually and vary widely, but for a sole proprietorship (in the U.S.) you're looking at around $100/year. L.L.C.s and Corporations range from a few hundred dollars into the thousands.

Fire inspections - Will you require fire inspections and will it cost you? Your municipality may require it for your licensing application and your insurance company may as well. Consider the costs needed for fire extinguishers and the like, as set out in your municipality's regulations.

Insurance - You will require liability insurance in many cases when leasing a commercial space or otherwise conducting business. Determine what the minimum amount of liability you need and contact a notable broker to find the best rates. These days, you may find a lot of this online. Many governing bodies will ask for proof of insurance. You may also require life, health or disability insurance.

Security - Often a liability insurance policy will require the business have minimal security measures in place, like bars over windows, a security system, etc. You may want this regardless as a good counter-measure. Security systems usually entail an installation fee, coupled with monthly monitoring costs.

Merchant setup and rental fees - If choosing to set up a merchant account so that you can accept debit and credit cards, the associated setup fees are either often bundled together or simply paid monthly. As mentioned earlier, scrutinise those contracts to know all the hidden costs. They can cost businesses hundreds of dollars per month in fees.

Phone/Internet hookup fees - Although typically reasonable, business phone lines cost more than residential, even when there is no notable difference in the service package. Typical costs can range anywhere from $50-$200 for initial installation.

Accountant - Depending on the business structure of your business, this may not be an optional expense. Business accounting and taxes can get very complicated, and a diligent accountant will have your back through it. You may require weekly bookkeeping services as well if you cannot stay on top of organising and managing your income and expense records. Costs can range from a few hundred to over a thousand dollars a year. Tax time alone can be from $500 and up.

Stationary - Common costs like this are usually low but can add up depending on your needs. Receipt books, printer ink, paper, pens, etc.

Advertising - Whichever advertising options you choose, try and set aside as many months worth as possible, as it may take some time to see a return on your investment. As you get going, other advertising opportunities will likely become available, and having the reserves to take advantage of them will allow you to reap the benefits.

Signage - Signage will vary in price depending on your needs and requirements. Depending on your building, you may need to comply with the owner's requests in how you display your sign or the style in the signage itself. Simple vinyl signs can be ordered online for under $100 and shipped right to your door. Conventional lighted signage may be in the thousands.

Lawyer - If you require a lawyer, they can run over $100/hour. If you want contracts that will hold up in court you're going to drop some serious coin to get them.

YOUR POLICIES

Thinking about your policies ahead of time will save you from being caught in a precarious position with a customer. The best time to establish your policies is during the planning stage and while writing your business plan and will help avoid making costly mistakes while facing your customers.

Think about all the circumstances that can come up and write them down in a notebook. Then decide how you will handle the situation and document that. Make a copy and if you're planning on working with others, turn it into a policy manual that can be referred to by anyone requiring it. I'll list some examples for you. Write down what you would do or offer your customer should any of these problems arise. These will also help you establish some systems of prevention.

Guitar Repair Policies

- Do you have a warranty on your work? If so, for how long? On what conditions?
- Customer unhappy with service/work received.
- Customer says it's worse than before they brought it in.
- The customer doesn't like the way it plays.
- The customer doesn't like the way the feels.
- Customer says you scratched it.
- Customer says it's rattling since you worked on it.
- Customer says the guitar is buzzy a week (or month or year) after having it in the shop.
- Guitar can't be setup due to non-functioning truss-rod, warped neck or other.
- Guitars' playability cannot be improved due to the non-functioning truss rod, warped neck or other.
- Guitar top cracks open while in your possession.
- Repaired cracked acoustic top splits open again after a year being in your shop.
- The customer wants free strings.
- The customer wants to barter.
- The customer wants you to give them a deal or discount on your labour.
- The customer wants a quantity discount (ex. 2-for-1).
- The customer can't pay.
- The customer doesn't return for the instrument, cannot contact the customer.
- The customer thinks it's too expensive, doesn't want to pay the bill.
- The customer won't pick up their instrument.
- The customer wants you to do something you haven't done before/ don't have the tools to do, etc.

Generic Retail Policies

Types of Payment
- What forms of currency do you accept?
- What information is required from a customer paying by cheque?
- Do you extend credit or offer terms to customers?
- How do you handle returned cheque?
- Which credit cards do you accept?
- How much money will you keep in the till?

Product Pricing
- What is your store's markup?
- Have you created a pricing strategy?
- Do you offer discounts on bulk purchases?
- Do you offer employee discounts?

Layaway
- Will you allow layaway purchases?
- How much will the customer be required to pay down?
- How long do you allow items to remain on layaway?
- Where will you store layaway items?
- What kind of system will you use to track layaways?

Returns and Exchanges
- Do you offer returns or exchanges?
- How liberal are you on returns and exchanges?
- In what condition should the merchandise be returned?
- Is there a time period for which an item may be refunded or exchanged?
- Will you require proof of purchase before exchanging or refunding?
- What data will you collect from the customer on the Merchandise Return Form?
- Where will your return policy be posted?

Special Orders
- Will you special order merchandise for customers?
- How much, if any, will you require as a deposit?
- What will you do if the customer doesn't return to pick up the item?

Hours of Operation
- What are the normal hours of operation?
- Will you have extended hours during the holiday shopping season?
- What holidays will the store close?

Other Store Policies and Procedures
- Who will be responsible for the general housekeeping of the store?
- What's the policy for groups soliciting donations?
- How will you handle product loss due to damage or theft?
- What is your shoplifting policy and procedures?

- What customer service practices will your store incorporate?
- Does your store provide delivery service?
- What will you do in the event of a power failure?

These examples should get you rolling. Try to imagine yourself as the customer when contemplating these policies. If you have prior retail experience, they will probably be easy for you to determine adequate outcomes, as you've seen various examples in action. If you have not, it's best to consider what's fair for both parties, and remember that you're in business to make money - not give business away. Your policies will allow you to enforce your rules confidently. As your business grows and you gain more experience, you can periodically revise your policies as necessary.

ACCOUNTING SYSTEMS & RECORD KEEPING

There are a few ways to keep your business activity organised, and it's highly recommended that you do. If you ever run into any problems, and you didn't keep any work or accounting detail, you will be the one at a loss. Record everything as you go, and you'll always be covered should you have any need to check back.

If you plan on running a legit business, you'll need a receipt system. You may choose to use a computer-based system that you can print off, or simply use the old-fashioned, yet effective, pen and receipt book method. If using the latter, choose a receipt book in triplicate from a stationary store like Staples. Having triplicate receipts allows one copy for the customer, one for your bookkeeping, and one that remains in your accessible records. If you buy the full-page size sales order books, you have plenty of room to write service details and these can also serve as your work order, killing two birds with one stone. Since you're taking service orders, some work order system will be beneficial. Perhaps you can remember what your customer's request is, but it can be easy to forget a detail or two. Having a work order present allows you to note everything the customer says, as well as make notes about the instrument yourself. For example, taking notes before and after is a great way to record your work and any changes you made to the instrument. The customer can see my specifications and adjustments you've made. It gives them a sense of confidence not only in your professionalism but also that those adjustments were actually made. Keeping in mind, although rare, you will have customers that can't actually tell you did a superb setup on their guitar. Perhaps they have a low skill level or don't play often. Work order and receipts can be custom ordered through a print company, having all pertinent information and company info displayed as you see fit. They can be expensive and aren't recommended for low operating costs, but cool non-the-less. Check the templates for record keeping at the end of this chapter or download from my website at *www.learn-guitar-setups.com/grb-downloads.*

Another record you will want to keep is the condition of the guitar. It hasn't happened to me thankfully, but I do know of customers that have insisted the guitar tech dented or scratched their guitar, in cases where they did not. What would you do in this situation, should it arise? If you did a scan of the instrument before working on it, you would find any notable markings that can be quickly jotted down. Sometimes I will even do this in front of the customer and discuss the blemishes.

Of course, there is the rare happening of *actually* scratching or denting a customers' guitar. Accidents do happen, and this line of work is not very forgiving, unfortunately. Let me be the first to tell you, learn to fix these sorts of things before you get started. Dents can be repaired or filled. Scratches can be buffed out. Always protect your customers' guitars with padding, rags/cloths, and shielding.

Methods of Payment
What methods of payment will you accept? These days, not many people carry cash or even want to. A credit card may be an option and a good one if you don't mind paying 3% of every transaction or more for that service. A popular way to accept credit cards is using a **mobile card reader** that attaches to your Smartphone. As an example, I've used one from Squareup, and the signup process is quick and easy. The readers work well, accepts most cards and funds are deposited in your bank account next day. They didn't require any credit checks and offer low rates (somewhere around 2.65% at the time of writing). Alternatively, setting up a merchant account with a bank to accept debit and credit cards is the most beneficial for your customer, and will appear more professional. Ultimately they may spend more money in your business with convenient payment options. Merchant accounts are convenient, but they do come with a big cost, one that may or may not be worthwhile for you. Every transaction will take a cut of your profits, and each type of payment is often a different cut. There are rental or lease fees, accounting or

admin fees and minimal transaction fees. There are plenty of choices, and competition has brought a lot of these costs down some, but be wary of hidden costs and contractual commitments. There may be high early-exit costs and other surprises. Many of these companies will be broken down into two or more customer service departments, so communicating with them, when you need help, can be a frustrating experience with little resolve. For example, one company I was with kept billing me rental charges far past my service agreement. Even after cancelling my services, I couldn't actually get through to the right department who was charging me; one agent would send me one way; another would send me back. After two days of my life wasted dealing with this, I still had gotten nowhere, so I had to close my bank account to stop the charges. Moral of the story, do a lot of research before signing anything. Sign with a reputable company. The one which is cheapest and most convenient may cost you a lot more down the road.

In Canada, we have **Interac Email Transfer**, an excellent option for customers who simply want to pay cash from bank to bank. It works similarly like a direct debit from their account into yours, all initiated through email and online banking.

Business Expense Receipts

Every time you spend money on your business, be it office supplies, strings or batteries, always keep your receipts. Just about at every turn, you will be spending money on supplies and tools. At tax time, all of your costs will offset your income, which will lower the amount of income tax potentially owed. If you have a vehicle, your vehicle costs including gas, maintenance and repairs can be written-off (to the percentage that you use it for business use). You can also write-off business use of the home if you have an office or otherwise doing any work there. Again, it will amount to a fraction of the costs as compared to the SQ footage that you use for business. If you have four rooms in the house and you use one, that will be 25% of your bills, rent, mortgage payments, insurance, etc. It all adds up significantly, and I urge you to take full advantage of the allowances that are granted by your governing tax body. If another business also employs you, don't discredit the importance of saving your receipts. Some of that income tax you pay through that employer may be making its way back to you, if you can show a loss in your business. Spend an hour with an accountant and he or she will fill you in on all the allowances and benefits.

MARKETING

Before getting thick into advertising, let's look at your marketing strategy. Do you have one? What is that exactly? Isn't it the same thing?

Marketing is the action of promoting and selling products or services, including market research and advertising. Simply put, marketing is the strategy behind selling your services, and products. Let's break this down.

Define yourself.
Define yourself and your business's services and products (if applicable), then show how the benefits you provide set you apart from your competition.

> *"Target audiences have become extremely specialised and segmented. No matter your industry, from restaurants to professional services to retail clothing stores, positioning your product or service competitively requires an understanding of your niche market. Not only do you need to be able to describe what you market, but you must also have a clear understanding of what your competitors are offering and to be able to show how your product or service provides a better value."*

Define your mission statement.
Having a mission statement aligns your intentions with your day-to-day actions and activities. It publicly communicates your intentions and shows your customers the dedication you have in your business. A Mission Statement for your business could be something like:

> *" To offer custom solutions, top quality work, and full range repair services to each and every one of my clients and their diverse needs, on a one-on-one basis.*
>
> *To always be willing to grow and learn and reinvent what my idea is of quality, service and value.*
>
> *To stay on top of current technology and education to make my work more efficient and valuable."*

Describe your target audience.
Your target market may be pretty broad, for example, m/f 18+, guitar, bass, ukulele players worldwide, etc.

Define your business goals.
What do you want to achieve? For example, are you hoping for a 20 percent increase in customers/jobs/sales every six months? Do you want to hit a certain revenue amount by a predetermined time? Write down a short list of goals—and make them measurable so that you'll know when you've achieved them (this is key so that you can identify *when* you hit your marks).

Define the strategies and tactics you'll use.
Your strategy is how you tie in your advertising ideas with the definition of your business to reach your goals. For example, list out your advertising plans and schedule with any promotional strategies over a predetermined time frame. Include your expectations from your efforts.

Set your budget.
You'll need to devote an amount of money to your first marketing initiate as well as a percentage of your revenues to your ongoing initiatives. Determining the costs of advertising ahead of time

will help you decide on how much will be required to spend so that it is effective. For example, you may choose to spend $25/m on Facebook ads until you reach a predetermined audience or measurable return on investment.

The key in marketing is never to stop, be it through monthly email newsletters, Facebook, website development or what have you. You don't need to be always spending advertising dollars, but working on your marketing is a daily/weekly endeavour. Also remember to ask all your new customers where they heard of you. Doing so help you isolate what is effective and what is not.

Here're a few ideas you can employ in your guitar repair business:
Advertising through local awareness campaigns, offering coupons, loyalty cards, discount cards, refer-a-friend discounts, or time-limited sales or promotions. More specific tactics could be something like offering free restringing or setups, with the purchase of a set of strings.

Don't forget some less obvious advertising methods like custom merchandise (shirts, straps, picks, branded guitars/kits, etc.). Making it for sale or giving it away is a great way to spread awareness of your business. Often guitar-playing communities are tightly knit, and word travels fast. If you have some cool merchandise, everyone will want a piece.

ADVERTISING

As mentioned previously, the nature of operating a service business is focusing on gaining new customers. The best advice I can give you is to advertise, advertise, advertise. In what ways can you do this?

If you're running a small operation, costs are going to be a major factor in how you can advertise. Where I live, Kijiji (a free online classified website) is very effective, and it doesn't cost anything unless I promote my ads (which I do, and it works). Perhaps you have something like that. Some businesses will focus on Facebook or place ads in newspapers. I've found, being that guitar repair is a small niche' business, usual advertising strategies didn't work so well (not to say you shouldn't try them). I have found, every method is *very* specific to a locality, meaning, what works in Edmonton (where I live), does not work in Vancouver. You need to test out what works and what doesn't.

Your website
Your website is your hub and primary calling card. This is where you should focus your online presence and invest your time in creating rich content including photos, videos and educational articles for today's DIY community. Also, you want to capture as many email address as you can, to add to your mailing list but don't go about it assertively. People are sick and tired of the noisy and flashy websites with all the pop ups asking for their email address. Just make a great looking, simple site and invite them to join *your community*.

Facebook
If you decide on building a Facebook business page, you may or may not know that for it to be effective, you must invest time regularly, creating posts and interacting with your audience. Today's Facebook algorithms require constant user activity to be seen by your captured audience. Consider this a daily endeavour. If you don't enjoy doing this, I'd suggest skipping it all together. These changes on Facebook has frustrated many businesses after investing years of growing a sizable audience. Even still, some are forced to pay for advertising or sponsored posts to be seen by their already-captured fans. Doesn't make sense to me personally, and is the reason why I won't use it much anymore.

Word of mouth
The most effective method of advertising is word of mouth. Do great work, and people will talk you up. Do something extraordinary, and you will gain a legion of die-hard fans. I once repaired a client's broken-in-half SG so well, that there was not even a trace that it was ever broken. His entire band was astonished by the work, and I've seen that customer back time and time again and granted I have received many referrals because of that as well. I also showcased the job on my website for all potential new customers to witness the extent of my work.

Showcase your work
If you build a website or Facebook page, post pictures of the work you do. Make videos, set up a Youtube account and offer some free advice.

Promo ideas
Get some great-looking cards made up and leave them with every guitar you touch. Offer discounts or a loyalty program (such as 10% off next visit or buy ten packs of strings, receive 1 for free), always give them a reason to return. Try and always include some padding in your pricing to offer discounts and specials. I have offered a "10% off" promo for pro-level musicians and students alike. People love getting deals.

Spread the word
When starting out, you will need to have patience while you build your business. It can take some time to get the word out. Locally focused social media posting can help. Have your family and

friends help spread the word. If there are any guitar stores who *don't* offer repairs, put up a poster and leave your cards. Go out to live shows and approach guitar players with your cards. Offer them a deal, being that they're professionals and let's face it, need all the breaks they can get.

Endorsements
If you know any local national celebrities, it goes without saying that you should approach them for an endorsement that you can use on all your advertising materials. If you don't know of anyone, consider approaching some while they're on tour. You can offer your services for free in exchange of a testimonial, and you just may be surprised that they take you up on it. Many national touring acts can't afford a road crew these days, having one or two people doing everything is more common and sure to have some compromises. Out of those that are roadies, you might be surprised how many of them know nothing more than how to restring and tune a guitar. Put your expertise to the tests and you may even get a road gig out of it.

Print Ads
Run a classified ad in the newspaper. Ads are usually more affordable than paying for a full advertisement in the editorial sections of the paper. Some entertainment papers or mags may offer some specials as well.

Adwords
AdWords is an advertising service by Google for businesses wanting to display ads on Google and its advertising network. These are the ads you see at the top of the page when you do a search. The AdWords program enables businesses to set a budget for advertising and to pay only when people click the ads. The ad service is relatively easy to setup, requiring some short sales copy and picking target keywords. If you are considering this,

Customer Testimonials
Another very effective method of advertising is showcasing customer testimonials. How many times have you shopped for something online and made a purchase based off of the customer testimonials? It can work the same way for you. My website has always been the focus of my advertising efforts through SEO strategies, writing blog posts, customer testimonials, links to social media, etc., essentially being my online calling card.

Your sales pitch
With that said, you'll want strong sales copy on your website and advertising materials. Sales copy is the text you use to persuade your audience to take a specific action. This copy may be used in sales emails, on web pages or in sales brochures. The ability to write great sales copy is one of the most important marketing skill you can learn and develop. Take a look at similar businesses and check out their copy.

WEBSITE COPY EXAMPLE

The following is an example of the kind of copy you'll want to consider on your website.

"Guitarworks" is an independent guitar repair and custom shop located in Your Town, State, Country. We offer one-on-one customer service for the student and professional alike. Free evaluations, instrument drop off's and pick ups are **by appointment**, to serve you better!

<u>Why Choose Us?</u>

- **Excellent Service** – We will take the time to get the job done right.
- **Lifetime Guarantee*** - This requires big...faith in the work we do!
- **Fast Turnarounds** – Smaller jobs are often finished within the week.
- **Quality Work** – satisfaction guaranteed backed by many years of experience
- **Complimentary Follow-up Maintenance** – Free tweaks to keep your axe in the same shape as it left the shop!
- **Fender Certified Technician** – And servicing all other makes, all models too. You name it; we fix it.
- **One-on-one Appointment** - Taking the time to determine the best solutions for you and your budget.
- **Consignment Sales**
- **Pick-up and Drop-Off Services** - Weekly deliveries available for a nominal fee
- **Rush Service Available -** For anyone needed immediate service

*See in store for details. Lifetime Guarantee on all work rendered and materials used for repairs, referring to any work performed that has not been tampered, adjusted, or changed through negligence, including environmental conditions, or direct intention from the condition it was in last when leaving the shop. Each manufacturer guarantees any aftermarket items if used. Brands, trademarks, service marks and copyrights addressed on this website are the property of their respective owners

This copy hits a lot of areas. I'll comb over the details that are pertinent. For starters, it designates where the business is located, stating that it is an independent shop. There is a market of people that don't like shopping big-box retailers, so they may be more inclined to try the independent alternative. It states what the business does (repair and custom work) and suggests a personal touch they may not find elsewhere (one-on-one). It invites people in for free evaluations, so there is no real gamble in coming in. Then it goes on to list all the reasons to choose them. Overall there is a real sense of commitment to service and an easy choice for a potential new customer. This company is focused on gaining new customers, which is apparent in this copy.

PRESS RELEASES

Another method of advertising sometimes overlooked by small businesses is to write a Press Release to announce the opening of your business. A press release, news release, media release, press statement or video release is a written or recorded communication directed at members of the news media for the purpose of announcing something newsworthy. Typically, they are faxed or emailed to editors and journalists at newspapers, magazines, radio stations, online media, or television stations.

A noteworthy quote from Hubspot, *"while it may be tempting to craft a press release that embellishes your company's accomplishments or twists the facts to make a story sound more intriguing to the media, remember: Press releases live in the public domain, which means your customers and prospective customers can see them. So instead of thinking of a press release solely as a ticket to earning news coverage, you should also think of it as a valuable piece of marketing content."*

So besides writing solely about the opening of your business, a story intertwined with, and the colouring of what you or your business is about, will be much more attractive to the press. And as you can imagine, that will also draw prospective customers your way. Free advertising!

Some of these common structural elements of a Press Release include:

- **Headline** – used to grab the attention of journalists and briefly summarise the news.
- **Dateline** – contains the release date and usually the originating city of the press release. If the date listed is after the date that the information was sent to the media, then the sender is requesting a news embargo, which journalists are under no obligation to honour.
- **Introduction** – first paragraph in a press release that gives basic answers to the questions of who, what, when, where and why.
- **Body** – further explanation, statistics, background, or other details relevant to the news.
- **Boilerplate** – a short "about" section, providing independent background on the issuing company, organisation, or individual.
- **Close** – in North America, traditionally the symbol "-30-" appears after the boilerplate or body and before the media contact information, indicating to media that the release has ended. A more modern equivalent has been the "###" symbol. In other countries, other means of indicating the end of the release may be used, such as the text "ends".
- **Media contact information** – name, phone number, email address, mailing address, or other contact information for the PR or other media relations contact person.

PRESS RELEASE TEMPLATE, NEW BUSINESS EXAMPLE

Contact Information:

[Company/Individual]
[Contact info]

[Small Business] Offers **[Product, Discounts, Event, etc.]**

FOR IMMEDIATE RELEASE

[City, State] – Local business **[name of business]** is please to offer **[product, discounts, event, etc.]**, for **[reason]**, beginning **[date]**.

[Details about what the small business is offering].

[More details, if necessary, perhaps including what benefit this offer will give to consumers].

[Possible quote from someone in the business, and/or a customer benefitting from this offer]

[Boilerplate – Company Info].

***

SERVICE PRESS RELEASE TEMPLATE

Contact Information:

[Company/Individual]
[Contact info]

[New Service] Coming from **[Company/Corporation]**

FOR IMMEDIATE RELEASE

[City, State] – **[Company/Corporation]** will be turning the **[industry]** world on its head with the launch of **[new service]**, a new service that **[description of what service will do, such as stream video, offer a new gaming platform, etc.]**. When **[new service]** starts up on **[date]**, **[specific target audience]** won't know what hit it.

[New service] will be **[an exciting addition to the industry, the first of its kind, etc.]**, and will offer **[more details on what, exactly, this new service will do]**.

[More details about this service, perhaps including pricing tiers, available upgrades, any special offers, etc.]

[Possible quote from someone related to the service, or from a critic or early adopter who has used the service and loved it].

[Boilerplate – Company Info].

***

CONCLUSION

With the information I have presented throughout this guide, you should be well on your way to the planning stages of your guitar repair business. This information is your starting point, as no two business operate the same. Use the resources at the back of this book and take the time to envision and plan the development of your business. I wish you the greatest successes, whether big or small, and all the best throughout your entrepreneurial journey.

RESOURCES

Tools List

Here is a list of some of the more common tools needed when setting up shop. There are plenty of speciality tools available, so consider this a basic, must-have tools list, and by no means comprehensive. You'll likely be always buying tools for one job or another. In no particular order or importance:

- Screwdriver set
- Precision screwdriver set
- Truss rod wrenches (multiple sets)
- Allen key sets
- Precision Straightedge(s)
- Gauged Saws
- Feeler gauge set(s)
- Nut and saddle vice
- Double-edge fret crowning file(s)
- Fret Rocker
- Precision/digital calliper
- Luthier's file set
- Bridge pin hole reamer(s)
- Fret Cutters
- Soldering iron
- 3rd hand
- Wire strippers
- Wire cutters
- Hemostat
- Pliers
- Side cutters
- Solder sucker
- Cam clamps
- Fret pressing system(s)
- Fret press insert (set)
- Fret press caul
- Multi-meter
- Double-edge Nut file (set)
- Neck support cauls
- Fret / Fingerboard levelling bar(s)
- 3" Fret leveller file
- 6" Fret leveller file
- Fretting Hammer
- Fret end dressing file
- 3-Corner file
- Precision file set
- Bridge pin hole slotting saw(s)
- Radius gauges
- Soundhole Clamps
- Nut and saddle shaping files
- Nut-slotting file (set)
- Under-string radius gauges
- Micro Chisels
- String spacing ruler
- String action gauge
- Fret tang nipper
- Precision chromatic tuner (strobe)
- String winder
- Socket set/socket drivers
- Drill bit set
- Fretguards
- Jigs and routing templates

Supplies List

Common shop supplies include:

- Selection of glues including white, wood, hide, fish, cyanoacrylate (with whip tips, solvent and accelerator)
- Selections of tape including light-tack masking, drafting, electrical, binding, etc.
- Naphtha/lighter fluid
- Cleaners, polishes
- Lemon oil
- Buffing compounds
- Wax, paste wax
- Rags, cotton rags, microfiber cloths
- Goggles
- Dust mask
- Rubber/latex gloves
- Paper towels, shop towels
- Fretwire (multiple sizes)
- Bone nut blanks
- Synthetic nut blanks (Graphtech, etc.)
- Strings
- Guitar mat and neck rest
- Abrasives (multiple grades/types)
- Sandbags

Equipment & Fixtures List

Here is a short list of possible equipment and fixtures you may need when setting up your shop.

- Lamps, lighting
- Workbench with carpeted/protected top
- Lumber/building supplies
- Slatwall
- Guitar hangers, guitar stands
- Sitting stools
- Computer
- Phone
- Fax
- Printer
- Fire extinguisher(s)
- Shop vac
- Guitar jig *(visit www.learn-guitarsetups.com/grb-downloads for instructions on how to build your own)*
- Guitar vice
- Bench vice
- Grinder
- Drill Press
- Belt/Disc Sander
- Beer fridge
- Band saw
- Spray equipment
- Compressor
- Spray booth
- Test amplifiers

Service Pricing Sheet EXAMPLE #1

Setups
Full setups include some or all of the following: Clean, check/adjust hardware, electronics, polish fretboard, oil if needed, restring, adjust the truss rod, action, bridge, neck, nut slots filed/lubed, pickup height & intonation set. **Fret dressing/resetting extra**

- Electric guitar setup $85
- Locking tremolo guitar $100
- Acoustic guitar setup $75
- 12 String guitars add $25
- Guitars in poor shape needing a lot of work to play properly are billed out per hour

Maintenance, adjustments, misc installs etc

- Humidity treatment $30
- Intonation on electric guitar $30/$50 (F.R
- Block off tremolo $30
- Restring & clean guitar $30
- Tuner installation, retrofit $30
- Tuner installation with reaming/drilling $75
- Stratocaster pickguard mounting $75

Custom nuts
Custom bone nuts are hand cut and shaped to fit your instrument; labour does not include the cost of required setup. Includes careful removal of old nut, manufacture, slot, install, and polish new nut.

- New custom guitar or bass nut $75
- New custom 12-string guitar nut $100
- Custom mandolin nuts $100
- Pre-cut, pre-slotted TUSQ or Graphtec nut Installation $20-$50 (with setup)
- Install Fender LSR or Floyd-style locking nut $100

Acoustic guitar bridges & saddles
Pricing does not include cost of setup

- Bone saddle hand-cut/shaped/polished $75
- Bone saddle intonated hand-cut/shaped/polished $100
- Pre-cut TUSQ or Graphtec saddle - $ included with setup
- Bridge removal and re-glue (bridge separating from top) starts at $150
- Installation and setup of JLD Bridge Doctor (to counteract a bellied guitar top) $75
- Fill and re-cut bridge slot $120
- Bridge shave $50

Electric guitar bridges

- Mount new hard-tail bridge, retrofit $30
- Mount new tremolo system, retrofit $75
- Mount & setup Hipshot Tremsetter Tremolo or Tremol-no Stabilizer $75
- Install new hardtail style bridge, non-retrofit (plugging/redrilling) $150
- Route out & install Floyd Rose/ floating bridge $250

SERVICE PRICING SHEET EXAMPLE #1 cont.

Electronics
- Pickup installation, retrofit $30 + $15 each one thereafter
- Install & setup Roland midi pickup $75
- Acoustic guitar pickup (under saddle) install $75 (requires setup)
- Acoustic soundhole pickup install (with endpin installation) $75
- Mandolin pickup/bridge install $100
- Control pot or 3-way switch replacement $30 + $15 each one thereafter
- Re-solder electronics starts at $20
- Stratocaster style switch replacement $45
- Guitar shield control cavity starts at $75
- Total re-wire start at $75
- Re-wire archtop / hollowbody guitar starts at $150
- Archtop pickup/parts replacement add $75 onto standard costs
- Pickup potting (wax dip) $30ea

Fretwork
A fret dressing is recommended when frets have become worn out in areas, and it's playability has suffered (ex. buzzing out in areas). Other times due to natural shifting of the wood, the frets become no longer uniformly level. A discerning player may choose to get his/her new guitar dressed because of the imperfections of a factory setup, and after the initial settling-in period, it will likely need it. When dressing the frets, all frets are seated and levelled to uniform height across the neck, re-shaped and polished.

A **refret** is necessary when frets are worn out and need to be replaced. Frets are removed, the neck is checked for straightness, re-surfaced when necessary, new frets are pressed in, assured to be levelled to a uniform height, reshaped and polished. Finish work extra. Costs do not include restring & setup.

- Full fret dressing starts at $150
- Minimal/spot fret dressing $75
- Glue and seat loose frets $50
- Refret unbound, non-lacquered necks $300
- Refret bound, non-lacquered neck $350
- Refret lacquered neck $375-$450
- Partial refret $15 per fret plus fret dressing and setup costs
- Filing fret ends (filing sharp frets from the neck drying out and shrinking) starts at $20
- Full fret end dressing and polish $45

Structural
- Glue and cleat cracked acoustic top $75
- Glue loose braces start at $50
- Seal cracked acoustic guitar bridge $30
- Reglue broken headstock with minimal touch-up $150
- Repair neck break/ splintered neck starts at $150
- Neck Press (for warped necks) starts at $50

Touch-ups & refinishes
- Buff out topical scratches starts at $30
- Drop-fill dings start at $75
- Paint touch-up and buff start at $75
- Refinish over neck or body starts at $250

Custom shop
All project guitars (aka Frankenstrats, mix and matched, etc.), custom guitar routing, parts installation, building & electronics are billed out at $75/hour shop rate. Definitive labour costs cannot be estimated due to the nature of the work required.

- Assemble electric guitar kits or custom guitar projects start at $250
- Replace/ install new bolt-on neck w/hardware start at $150
- Install pickguard, pickups, electronics, hardware, wire-up starts at $150

Service Pricing Sheet EXAMPLE #2

Precision Guitar and Bass Setups w/ Add-ons

Setup prices:
- Hard-tails $65
- Tremolo's $75
- Locking tremolos $100
- Acoustic guitar, ukulele setup from $50
- 12-string guitars add $30
- Mandolins, banjo's $75
- Intonation only $30/ locking tremolo $45
- Adjust action (truss rod/string height at bridge only) $35/ locking tremolo $50

Additional costs w/ setups:
- Guitars needing a lot of work to be made playable will be billed hourly.
- Neck removal (truss rod access or shim) $10
- Add string tree $6ea
- Remove, shim & re-cut nut $15
- Fill & re-cut nut slots $6ea
- Extra dirty guitar and/or stickers removed $15
- Block tremolo one-way w/ hardwood $20
- Block tremolo (full) w/ hardwood $30
- Tuner install $35 (retrofit w/restring)
- Tuner installation w/ reaming/drilling $75

Small Jobs
- Restring & clean $20 (+ strings)
- Plug/ redrill stripped strap pin $6ea
- Plug/ redrill small screw holes $1.25ea
- Humidity Treatment $30

Electronics
- Fine tune pickup pole pieces to string radius $6per pickup
- Replace dirty pots/switches (*see electronics)
- Replace jack $15+

Frets
- High frets seated & glued $8ea
- Sharp fret ends filed/dressed $45
- Frets re-bevelled and dressed for smooth, easy feel $45
- Fret level (light dressing/optimised for low action) $150
- Fret level (deep level, bad frets, neck) $250
- Fret level Stainless Steel $250
- Deluxe fret polish (all scratches out, polished sheen/smooth playing) $45

Acoustic Instrument Upgrades & Repairs

Upgrades
- Install strap pins $6ea
- Install under saddle pickup system $75 +pickup
- New custom nut $85
- New intonated compensated custom saddle $125
- Install/ setup JLD Bridge System Dr. (+ req. setup) $75
- Install soundhole pickup with endpin jack $65
- Install under saddle pickup w/ endpin (req setup) $75
- Mandolin pickup/bridge install $100
- Banjo Pickup Install $75
- Custom pickguard $45

Repairs *Pricing does not include cost of setup*
- New bone saddle, hand-cut, shaped and polished $75
- New bone saddle intonated, hand-cut, shaped and polished $120
- Pre-cut Graphtech saddle - $20
- Bridge removal and re-glue (bridge separating from top) starts at $150
- Seat & glue separating/ cracked bridge $35
- Fill and re-cut bridge slot for proper placement/ intonation $120
- Bridge shave $75
- Bracing repair $50, $35 thereafter
- Crack Repair w/ cleating $75+
- Humidity Treatment $30
- Pickup testing/ troubleshooting $35

SERVICE PRICING SHEET EXAMPLE #2 cont.
Electric Guitar Upgrades

Stratocaster-style upgrades
- Saddle upgrades for less noise/rattling $30
- New bone nut $85
- New TUSQ/ Earvana nut $30
- Control pot mod (customise tone controls to your liking) $45
- Block tremolo one-way w/ hardwood $20
- Block Tremolo (full) w/ hardwood $30
- Tone cap upgrades (change over to Orange Drop, oil-filled, etc.) $10ea
- Treble bleed mod $20 w/ other, $45 alone
- Additional switch (all pickups on/phase etc) $45
- Custom pickguards $75+

Telecaster-style upgrades/ add-ons
- New bone nut $85
- New TUSQ/ Earvana nut $30
- Drill down, wax bridge (prevent feedback) $35
- Feedback control (drill down & wax bridge, extra padding at bridge pickup) $40
- Add new saddles/compensated $30
- Reverse control plate $45
- Esquire mod $45
- Treble bleed mod $20
- Custom pickguards $75+

Pickups
- Potting/ re-potting/ dipping with removal/install/testing $75ea
- Potting/ dipping pickups alone $35ea
- Install new pickup (retrofit) $35, $15 thereafter
- Testing/diagnosing electronics/pickups $35+
- 18 Volt Mod (active pickups) $25
- 18 Volt Mod with routing for additional battery $85+

Electric guitar bridges
- Mount new hard-tail bridge, retrofit $30
- Mount new tremolo system, retrofit $75
- Mount & setup Hipshot Tremsetter tremolo or Tremol-no stabiliser $75 (Setup req.)
- Install new hardtail style bridge, non-retrofit (plugging/re-drilling) $150
- Route out & install Floyd Rose/ floating bridge $250

Gibson-style upgrades/ add-ons
- New bone nut $85
- New TUSQ/ Earvana nut $30
- Dress nut slots for less binding (string ping) $15
- 50's wiring mod $45
- Tone cap upgrades (change over to Orange Drop, oil-filled, etc.) $10ea
- Treble bleed mod $30 (x2)
- Custom pickguards $75+

"Import" electric guitar upgrades
- Dlx. fret polish, seat/glue and level frets
- Upgrade electronics (pots/switches)
- Upgrade h/w (bridge/saddle/tuners)
- Upgrade nut

Electronics pricing
- Clean/test only $15
- Install new pot $30, $15 thereafter
- Install new toggle switch $35
- Install new switch (blade/strat) $45
- Install new jack $15+
- Install complete set of controls $85+
- Fix solder joint(s) $6+
- Modify guitar for custom controls (route, drill, etc $75+
- Rewire a muck-up to functional $75 (no assembly)
- Total rewire (2 pots/switch) $75, additional switches $15ea
- Total rewire (3+ potentiometers/switch) $120, additional switches $15ea
- Install & Setup Roland Midi Pickup $75+ (setup req.)
- Guitar shield control cavity starts at $75 (removal/installation of pickups/hardware extra)
- Re-wire archtop /hollow-body guitar starts at $150
- Archtops pickup/parts replacement add $75

SERVICE PRICING SHEET EXAMPLE #2 cont.
Custom Work & Fretwork

Custom modifications	Custom nuts
<ul><li>Route pickup space only $50+, $35 thereafter</li><li>Route pickup space Les Paul/archtop $65+</li><li>Route control cavity space $75</li><li>Route /install 9 volt battery compartment $50</li><li>Route /install Floyd Rose recessed cavity (require pre-assembly) $250</li><li>Route / install Floyd Rose nut shelf $75</li><li>Route / install LSR roller nut $75</li><li>Dowel re-drill bridge posts / install (require pre-assembly) $150</li><li>Pickguard re-shaping for custom fitting $75</li><li>Custom pickguards $75+up</li></ul>	<ul><li>New custom guitar or bass nut $85</li><li>New custom 12-string guitar nut $120</li><li>Custom mandolin nut $100</li><li>Pre-cut, pre-slotted TUSQ or Graphtec nut installation $20-$50</li><li>Install Fender LSR or Floyd lock nut $100 (routing required)</li></ul>
Custom shop & routing<ul><li>Assemble, wire & setup electric guitar kits /custom guitar projects (ex. Warmoth) start at $300</li><li>Replace/ install new bolt-on neck + tuners start at $150</li><li>Install pickguard, pickups, electronics, hardware, wire-up only starts at $150</li><li>Routing pickup cavity $75 + $35 thereafter</li><li>Routing archtop/Les Paul $90 + $50 thereafter</li><li>Route battery box $50</li><li>Routing for Floyd Rose bridge $250 and nut $75</li></ul>**Structural repairs**<ul><li>Re-glue broken headstock starts at $150</li><li>Repair multiple neck breaks/ splintered neck starts at $250</li><li>Repair broken headstock with splicing $300+</li><li>Neck Press (for twisted necks) $60</li></ul>	**Fretwork** *Nut replacements and finish work extra. Costs do not include setup.*<ul><li>Full fret dressing starts at $150</li><li>Minimal fret dressing/ spot-dressing $75</li><li>Glue and seat loose frets $ 8ea or $50 w/ fret level</li><li>Refret unbound, non-lacquered necks $300</li><li>Refret bound, non-lacquered neck $350</li><li>Refret lacquered neck $375-$450</li><li>Partial refret $150 + $15 per fret (setup required)</li><li>Stainless steel frets upgrade add $120</li><li>Plane out neck twists/warps from $75</li><li>Filing sharp fret ends (fret bevel dressing & polishing) $45</li><li>Lacquer touch-up fretboard sides after refret $100</li><li>Neck Jig fretwork adds $100 (for squirrely/warped necks)</li></ul>
Finish touch-ups<ul><li>Buff out topical scratches starts at $35</li><li>Drop-fill dings start at $75</li><li>Paint touch-up and buff start at $75</li><li>Refinish over neck or body starts at $250</li><li>Touch-up fretboard sides after refret $112.50</li></ul>	**Amplifier & electronics**<ul><li>Re-tube and bias amplifier from $75</li><li>Replace guitar amplifier speakers $75 + $35 thereafter</li><li>Clean pots, replace parts $75/hr</li><li>Re-cap/ test</li></ul>**Misc**<ul><li>Packing/unpacking w/storage customer instruments $15</li></ul>

Work Order TEMPLATE #1

Here is an example of a work order that you can use in your shop. It was based on Dan Erlewines', who has offered it as a free download on his website www.danerlewine.com (with a few changes made for my own needs).

Work Order #

Date	_____	Rush Date/Fee	_____
Name	_____	Make	_____
Address	_____	Model	_____
	_____	Serial	_____
Phone	_____	Case	Hard Soft None
Email	_____		1 2 3 4 5 6 7 8 9
Add to mailing list? Yes / No		Condition	10
Technician	_____	String Gauge	_____
		Tuning	_____

Labour & Parts Estimate/ Work Order

This estimate is subject to change

Playing Style _____

Notes (bridge tilt, etc) _____

Description of Services Requested	Cost

Parts:	Cost

Less Deposit _____
Total $ _____

MAX. cost authorized by customer at time of sign-in: $ _____

Added services for completion:	Cost

Customer's Signature _____

ESTIMATES ARE FOR LABOR ONLY AND DO NOT INCLUDE COST OF SUPPLIES, PARTS, OR TAXES. WE WILL NOT BE HELD RESPONSIBLE
FOR LOSS OR DAMAGE CAUSED BY FIRE, THEFT, TESTING, OR ANY OTHER CAUSES BEYOND OUR CONTROL. TERMS - NET CASH.

NO INSTRUMENTS HELD OVER 30 DAYS

Work Order TEMPLATE #2 (Guitar Setup)

I get tonnes of setups, and I've always scrutinised over the process. I came up with this service sheet to help clarify and communicate what I do.

A Precision Setup consists of assessing instruments' playability, checking for neck twists, high/low frets, testing all functions, cleaning the guitar, polishing frets, tightening loose hardware, cleaning electronic components, restringing, adjusting truss rod (relief in neck), adjusting string height (at bridge & nut), adjusting bridge angle (where applicable), adjusting neck angle (where applicable), lubricating necessary components, and setting the intonation at the 12th fret on a precision virtual strobe tuner.

Sign-in notes:
_____
_____
_____
_____

	Playability assessment	N/A	OK
	Clean	N/A	OK
	Polish frets	N/A	OK
	Check/ tighten hardware	N/A	OK
	Check/ clean electronics	N/A	OK
	Restring	N/A	OK
	Adjust relief	N/A	OK
	Adjust neck tilt/ angle	N/A	OK
	Adjust bridge	N/A	OK
	Adjust string height	N/A	OK
	Dress nut slots	N/A	OK
	Adjust pickup height	N/A	OK
	Intonation	N/A	OK
	Custom requests	N/A	OK
	Lubricated	N/A	OK
	Tested	N/A	OK

Sign-out notes:
_____
_____
_____
_____
_____
_____

Guitar Setup Spec Sheet EXAMPLE

Here is a different version that is formatted to be more of a brochure. Specs are noted so that the customer can keep it with the guitar, or left in the guitar case. Easily to refer to, a different tech with adequate training could dial in the prior setup. I printed an article on truss rods on one page, to educate the customer about the nuances of adjustment and potential for readjustment. On the backside I printed a price list so that it was easy to refer to.

Precision Setup Spec Sheet

Guitar Make/Model	
Serial #	
Tuning	
String gauge	
Fretboard radius	
Relief setting	
String height at 12th	
String height at Nut	
Notes	

A Precision Guitar Setup consists of testing all functions, cleaning the guitar, polishing frets, tightening loose hardware, cleaning electronic components, restringing, adjusting truss rod (relief in neck), adjusting string height (at bridge & nut), adjusting bridge angle (where applicable), adjusting neck angle (where applicable), lubricating necessary components, and setting the intonation on a precision virtual strobe tuner. Your technician can discuss any concerns you have with your guitar and offer solutions afforded by your budget.

Business Startup Checklist

- Research the business idea
- What will you sell
- Who will buy it and how often
- Are you willing to do what it takes to sell yourself and the product
- What will it cost to produce, advertise, sell & deliver
- With what laws will you have to comply
- Can you make a profit
- How long will it take to make a profit
- Write a business plan and marketing plan
- Choose a business name
- Verify right to use the name
- See if the business name is available as a domain name
- Register the business name and get a business certificate
- Register your domain name even if you aren't ready to use it yet
- Choose a location for the business or make space in the house for it
- Check zoning laws
- File partnership or corporate papers if applicable
- Get any required business licenses or permits
- Reserve your corporate name if you will be incorporating
- Register or reserve state or federal trademark
- Register copyrights
- Apply for patent if you will be marketing an invention
- Order any required notices (advertisements you have to place) of your intent to do business in the community
- Have business phone or extra residential phone lines installed
- Order business cards
- Setup website & social media
- Check into business insurance needs
- Find out about health insurance if you will not have coverage from a spouse
- Open a business bank account
- Set up your accounting system
- Line up suppliers and service providers
- Work your network

Company Overview Example

"Guitarworks" is a new company that will provide quality musical instrument repair services & custom work, as well as new & used instruments, parts and equipment.

Our niche in the marketplace will be in the following areas:

- Excellent customer service, one-on-one service
- Educating our clients about the work that we do
- First-rate guitar repairs, setups and custom work
- Fast turnarounds whenever possible
- Same day/while-you-wait service
- Exclusive custom services
- Niche, in-house products & solutions
- Wide used equipment selection
- Wide parts selection
- DIY, BYO products & resources
- Luthier supplies & educational resources
- Strong internet presence for Intl. sales and branding
- Exclusive building and repair classes

These exclusive niche's set "Guitarworks" far apart from the competition - mostly by catering to the market who enjoy not only guitars and musical equipment but also those who enjoy building, modifying and customising them as well. People in the city have many choices for buying new musical instruments, but the customer service in these stores usually fall by the wayside in exchange for reaching high sales numbers. Used musical instrument choices in the city are limited to pawnshops or in the back corner of a few select stores. The city has not had a prominently used guitar store in the past ten years or more.

Primary advertising will be through a website, FB Page, Kijiji Ads, Weekly Rotating Ads and referrals through word of mouth.

WHAT WE SELL
- Repair services
- Custom services
- Classes & courses
- Used equipment
- New equipment, parts & accessories
- Custom built guitars and other stringed musical instruments
- DIY Resources and luthier supplies
- Consignment sales

WHO WE SELL TO
Our primary target market is m/f ages 12 year of age and up, guitar players of all experience level, guitar enthusiasts, and the DIY musical community.
- Locally (FB Stats approx. 60,000 + approx. 100,000 not on FB)
- Internationally via eBay, Reverb.com, Amazon

MISSION STATEMENT
To offer efficient, top quality work, and a wide range of musical instrument repair services to our clients and their diverse needs.

To be advocates for quality craftsmanship, whether in our own work or others

To offer solutions that put the luxury of a high-priced custom guitar into the hands of any individual.

To empower our clients through education and information.

One Page Business Plan

Answer each question with one or two short sentences

OVERVIEW
What will you sell?

_____

_____

Who will buy it?

_____

_____

How will your business idea(s) help people?

_____

MONEY
What will you charge?

_____

_____

How will you receive payments?

_____

_____

How else will you make money from this project?

_____

_____

HUSTLING
How will customers learn about your business?

_____

_____

How can you encourage referrals

_____

_____

SUCCESS
The project will be successful when it achieves these metrics: Number of customers

_____

_____

- or - annual net income

_____

_____

- or - *(other)*

_____

OBSTACLES/CHALLENGES
Specific concern #1

_____

_____

Proposed solution #1

_____

_____

Press Release EXAMPLE

Contact Information:

[Company/Individual]
[Contact info]

[New Service] Coming from **[Company/Corporation]**

FOR IMMEDIATE RELEASE

[City, State] – **[Company/Corporation]** will be turning the **[industry]** world on its head with the launch of **[new service]**, a new service that **[description of what service will do, such as stream video, offer a new gaming platform, etc.]**. When **[new service]** starts up on **[date]**, **[specific target audience]** won't know what hit it.

[New service] will be **[an exciting addition to the industry, the first of its kind, etc.]**, and will offer **[more details on what, exactly, this new service will do]**.

[More details about this service, perhaps including pricing tiers, available upgrades, any special offers, etc.]

[Possible quote from someone related to the service, or from a critic or early adopter who has used the service and loved it].

[Company Info].

***

Warranty Policy EXAMPLES

Here is a list of generic warranty policies to draw some inspiration from when creating your own.

Warranty of Repair Services and Used Items

- 90 Day Parts, Labour & Satisfaction Warranty, Extended Warranty available to cover parts and labour. Precision Setup included (valued at up to $120).
- Excludes used electronic items.

Warranty of Consignments/ Electronics

- 30 Day Defective Return Policy.

Warranty of New Items

- One year Parts & Labour Warranty, Extended Warranty available.

Extended Warranty

If you are interested in receiving this coverage, you have the option of purchasing additional years of the Extended Warranty. The pricing is as follows:

NEW products: 4% of selling price to double the warranty from 1 year to 2 years. 4% for each additional year. $10 minimum.

USED products: 4% of selling price to increase the warranty from 3 months to 1 year. 4% for each additional year. $10 minimum.

The value of the protection is limited to $1,500.00, and only provides a replacement instrument, no cash payout. The protection maximum remains $1,500 regardless of the number of extra years purchased or the selling price of the instrument. The $1,500 protection is effective immediately once additional Extended Warranty is purchased.

Notes: Used products come with a 3-month Extended Warranty. Some products (i.e. computers, software, cymbals) are covered only by the manufacturer's warranty. Consumables (i.e. strings, reeds, drum sticks, batteries, tubes, cross faders) are excluded as they are designed to be replaced. Willful or cosmetic damage is not covered. Speakers damaged by overpowering are generally not covered. Our coverage does not provide compensation for loss of use.

30 Day Return/Exchange Policy
If for any reason, you're not happy with your purchase, you can exchange it or return it for a full refund within 30 days of purchase, provided that it's in new condition and its original packaging. Exceptions - Special orders, computer software, print music, harmonicas, and earplugs/in-ear monitors. Any items purchased as a Christmas gift after November 1st will be accepted for return until January 15th.

"Guitarworks" reserves the right to amend this policy at our discretion.

Accounting Forms

Daily Sales Report

Date: _____

Cash	$_____
Checks	$_____
Master Card	$_____
Visa	$_____
Other	$_____
Store Credit	$_____
Subtotal	$_____
Starting Float (subtract)	$_____
Deposit Total	$_____
Returns	$_____
Voids	$_____
Pay Outs	$_____
Other	$_____
Total Cash Paid Out	$_____
Add Deposit Total & Total Cash Paid Out	$_____
Sales Tax Collected	$_____
Register Reading	$_____
Difference (+ or -)	$_____

Business Expense Worksheet (Canadian)

Name:
SIN:
TAX Year:

Total your expenses according to the following categories.

Revenue:
Less 5% GST
GST Collected
Revenue GST exempt

Total Revenue without GST

Cost of Goods Sold
Purchases
Subcontracts
Direct wages
Other costs of goods

Expenses:
Advertising and promotion
Bad debts
Licenses, dues, memberships & subscriptions
Insurance
Loan interest expense
Maintenance & repairs
Management & Adm fees
Meals and Entertainment (100%)
Supplies
Office and supplies
Professional fees (legal, accounting, etc.)
Rent & property taxes
Salaries, wages and benefits
Travel
Telephone, cell, internet
Convention fees
Private health care plan costs
Moving Expenses
Shipping

Capital Costs:
1
2
3

Auto Expenses:
KM personal _____
KM Business _____
Fuel (Gas and Oil)
Maintenance & repairs
Insurance
Loan interest
lease payments and lease terms
New Car? - Cost and details
Old Car - Sold for?
Less: Auto allowance received

Business Use of Home
Sq feet total
Sq feet business
Utilities
Insurance
Repairs & Maintenance
Mortgage interest
Property taxes
Rent
Condo fees

ABOUT THE AUTHOR

Since I was a boy, I've taken everything apart to learn how it works (often to my parents' distress). When I started playing the guitar, it was no different. I began customising them immediately to suit my tastes and preferences better. This led me to build guitars, which lead me to repair and custom work as a career.

After working in numerous places, I opened a shop of my own to better serve my clients and the guitar-playing community in my city. Now I hold classes on various aspects of repair, setups, and maintenance, which gives me an opportunity to share what I've learned along the way.

Also available by Jonny Blackwood in digital and print editions:

How to Setup Your Guitar like a Pro: An Easy Guide for Beginners

How to Build & Setup Guitar Kits like a Pro: An Easy Guide for Bolt-on Neck Guitars

* * * * *

NOTES

NOTES

Made in the USA
Coppell, TX
17 April 2020